To God Be The Glory For The Things He Has Done And Will Do
II

Michael R. Williams

ISBN 978-1-64114-622-7 (Paperback)
ISBN 978-1-64114-623-4 (Digital)

Copyright © 2017 by Michael R. Williams

All rights reserved. No part of this publication may be reproduced, distributed, or transmitted in any form or by any means, including photocopying, recording, or other electronic or mechanical methods without the prior written permission of the publisher. For permission requests, solicit the publisher via the address below.

Christian Faith Publishing, Inc.
296 Chestnut Street
Meadville, PA 16335
www.christianfaithpublishing.com

Printed in the United States of America

"May the words of my mouth
and the meditation of my heart be
pleasing in your sight, O Lord, my Rock
and my Redeemer."

PSALM 19:14

It's Not About Me

The Lord is my strength

He is my source of energy
The Father we have who we cannot see

He Blessed Me With

A Talent
A Gift
The Ability

To minister His Word through poetry

All Honor And Glory
Goes Directly To Thee

Let The Truth Be Told

It's Not About Me

In his heart a man plans his
course but the Lord determines his steps.

PROVERBS 16:9

The Lord is Our Strength

He is our source of energy
The Father we have who we cannot see

He Blessed Us All With

A Talent
A Gift
The Ability

He Does It For Us All
It's Not Just Me

All Honor And Glory
Goes Directly To Thee

We All Should Give Thanks To Our Father

Down On Our Knees

Thank You Lord

Blessed By The Best

These are the Words of Him
who is holy and true,
who holds the key of David.

What He opens no one can shut,
and what He shuts no one can open.
I know your deeds.

See, I have placed before
you an open door
that no one can shut.

I know that you have little strength,
yet you have kept My Word
and have not denied My name.

REVELATION 3:7-8

Dedication

This book is dedicated to all the people of this world.
We all need God in our lives today; because without God,
There Is No-Way!

I am the Lord, the God of all mankind. Is anything too hard for Me?
JEREMIAH 32:27

God is our refuge and strength, an ever-present help in trouble.
PSALM 46:1

He is the Rock His works are perfect, and all His ways are just.
A faithful God who does no wrong, upright and just is He.
DEUTERONOMY 32:4

Be strong and courageous. Do not be afraid or terrified because of
them, for the Lord your God goes with you; He will never leave
you nor forsake you.
DEUTERONOMY 31:6

Peter and the other apostles replied: We must obey God
rather than men!
ACTS 5:29

Jesus looked at them and said, "With man this is impossible, but
with God all things are possible."
MATTHEW 19:26

To God Be The Glory
AMEN & HALLELUJAH

GOD
"There Is No One Like You"

Acknowledgments

He's Number 1, He's Number 1, He's Number 1!!

I would like to first thank God our Father for who I am. Without Him I don't know where I would be. He's the one who made all this possible. He's our Father from above, The Father we have, who we All Should Love!!! (Everyone).

There is "Nothing He Can't Do", He helped me, He can surely help you.

Anything day or night, call on Him, He'll make things right.

PRAY DAILY

Thanks to Kathie Athy and Chris Athy for all they have done helping me to get things right. Thanks to my wife, kids, and everyone who was behind me 100% believing and supporting me along the way.

Thank You

God Bless

The Ten Commandments

EXODUS 20:1-17

People,

Here Are My Laws

Please *Do Not Ignore*
All the people of this world
Are who they are for

This is the way that life should be
Learn them, Live them
In Honor Of Me

My Laws were created for this world to do
Please give Me your best
That's All I Ask Of You

GOD

The Ten Commandments

I. Thou shall have no other gods before Me.

II. Thou shall not make unto thee any graven images.

III. Thou shall not take the name of the Lord thy God in vain.

IV. Remember the Sabbath day, to keep it Holy.

V. Honor thy father and thy mother.

VI. Thou shall not kill.

VII. Thou shall not commit adultery.

VIII. Thou shall not steal.

IX. Thou shall not bear false witness against thy neighbor.

X. Thou shall not covet.

Table of Contents

MATTHEW 22:37 2
Amen 3

HEBREWS 12:2 4
A True Friend 5

MATTHEW 6:25 6
Don't Worry About A Thing 7

ACTS 5:29 8
Father Knows Best 9

JOHN 14:6 10
Get High 11

ROMANS 8:30 12
God's Calling 13

PSALM 54:4 14
God's Got Your Back 15

ROMANS 10:9-10 16
Heaven Bound 17

HEBREWS 13:6 18
Help Me Jesus 19

LEVITICUS 19:18 20
Hungry For Revenge 21

MARK 10:9 22
Marriage: It's A Job 23

PSALM 119:35 24
Need Directions 25

JOSHUA 24:15 26
Now Is The Time 27

PSALM 118:1 28
Praise Him 29

I JOHN 3:3.. 30
The Answer 31

PSALM 51:10 32
The Heart 33

JOHN 10:10... 34
The Healer 35

MARK 11:24 36
The Power Of Prayer 37

PROVERBS 3:5-6... 38
Trust In The Lord
(Always Pray) 39

PSALM 30:12 40
Where Would I Be 41

HEBREWS 11:1 42
Without A Doubt 43

MATTHEW 3:17 44
Who Is This Man
(It Can Only Be).. 45

EPHESIANS 4:32 46
Who's Perfect. 47

DEUTERONOMY 1:17. 48
Who's The Judge 49

NAHUM 1:7 50
Why 51

Trust in the Lord with all your heart
and lean not on your own understanding;
in all your ways acknowledge Him,
and He will make your paths straight.

PROVERBS 3:5-6

To God Be The Glory

For The Things He Has Done

And Will Do!

II

Michael Williams

MESSAGES FROM GOD

To God Be The Glory

Amen

Jesus replied: Love the Lord your God with all your heart and with all your soul and with all your mind.

MATTHEW 22:37

But seek first His kingdom and His righteousness, and all these things will be given to you as well.

MATTHEW 6:33

Amen

"My people are destroyed from lack of knowledge."

HOSEA 4:6

Don't walk around Blind
Seek and you will Find

The place you need to Go

To Church

The Book you need to Know

The Bible

Do not let this book of the law depart from your mouth; meditate on it day and night, so that you may be careful to do everything written in it. Then you will be prosperous and successful.

JOSHUA 1:8

Go to Church
Know the Bible
AMEN

A True Friend

Let us fix our eyes on Jesus the author and perfecter of our faith, who for the joy set before Him endured the cross, scorning its shame, and sat down at the right hand of the throne of God.

HEBREWS 12:2

A True Friend

Troubled one don't you cry
Wipe that tear from your eye

Don't let life's problems bother you
It's not what happens but what you do

NEED HELP

I'm always here to comfort you
What do you need for Me to do

Just ask Me I can help you out
Helping people is what I'm all about

Have Faith Believe and Trust in Me
I can change your life I Guarantee

I'm A True Friend

And I'll Always Be

So don't worry about life's problems

Just Bring Them To Me

A True Friend

Jesus Christ

Faithful & True Witness

To God Be The Glory

Don't Worry About A Thing

Therefore I tell you, do not worry about your life, what you will eat or drink; or about your body, what you will wear. Is not life more important than food, and the body more important than clothes?

MATTHEW 6:25

Don't Worry About A Thing

Therefore I tell you, do not worry about your life.......

Matthew 6:25

My Child

I know what you're going through
Don't worry about your life
You Don't Have To

Worry

It's so powerful
It can tear you apart

Trust In Me
With All Your Heart

You can't control what the future will bring
Believe Me when I say

Don't Worry About A Thing

I Will Take Care Of You

GOD

Father Knows Best

Peter and the other apostles replied: "We must obey God rather than man!"

ACTS 5:29

"For I know the plans I have for you," declares the Lord, "plans to prosper you and not harm you, plans to give you hope and a future."

JEREMIAH 29:11

Father Knows Best

Our Father in Heaven...

MATTHEW 6:9-13

We think it's okay
Doing things our way
Not caring what our Father has to say

He tries to tell us how things should be
But often times we disagree

Children

I'm God your Father
I'm not like all the rest
Trust Me when I say

Father Knows Best

Trust is the Lord with all your heart and lean not on your own understanding; in all your ways acknowledge Him,
and He will make your paths straight.

PROVERBS 3:5-6

To God Be The Glory

Get High

Jesus answered,
I am The Way, and The Truth and
The Life.

John 14:6

Get High

Jesus Christ

He'll Get You High
He's an experience everyone should try

Young and old
Big or small

Jesus Christ
He's for us all

He doesn't taste like cocaine
He doesn't stink like pot
He doesn't smell like alcohol
Illegal He is not

When life's problems come your way
And you're tired of battling day after day

Drugs or Alcohol Don't You Try

Jesus Christ

He'll Get You High

God's Calling

And those He predestined He also called; those He called, He also justified; those He justified, He also glorified.

ROMANS 8:30

God doesn't call the qualified;
God qualifies the called.

God's Calling

Ring!   Ring!   Ring!

After the tone please leave a message

Anybody Home

Are you one of those chosen ones
To perform some task that God wants done

God's calling, is anyone there
Answer the phone or maybe you Just Don't Care

It's God again He keeps calling me
I'm afraid of what He wants
I wish He'd let me be

Don't be afraid when God calls on you
It's a guarantee He'll help you through

He makes our impossible possible to do
It's all about God it's not about you

So if your phone is ringing loud and clear
And you're pretending you're nowhere near
On your answering machine you will hear

Hi
This is God

I'm calling for you My chosen one
I have a task that needs to be done
Sometimes it will be tough and you will see
But through it all
You'll Still Have Me

GOD

God's Got Your Back

Surely God is my help;
The Lord is the one who sustains me.

PSALM 54:4

For The Things He Has Done And Will Do! Part II

God's Got Your Back

How's your Christian Walk
Has it turned into Just Christian Talk

The right things that you used to do
Life's problems are completely changing you

Why

Don't let this world get to you
No matter what you're going through

There's nothing in this world
That should get you off track

Just Remember

GOD'S GOT YOUR BACK

PSALM 46:1

God is our refuge and strength an
ever-present help in trouble

Stay on Track

GOD'S GOT YOUR BACK

Heaven Bound

That if you confess with your mouth, "Jesus is Lord," and believe in your heart that God raised Him from the dead,
you will be saved.
For it is with your heart that you believe and are justified, and it is with your mouth that you confess
and are saved.

ROMANS 10:9-10

Heaven Bound

This old world is fading fast we don't know how long it will last

There's one thing that's perfectly clear
Jesus is coming back
Will you be left here

Heaven Bound

What will happen to you
Do you truly have a clue

If you're serious about wanting to go **ROMANS 10:9-10** is what you must know

Get Saved

Confess & Believe

When it's time get off this ground

Don't Be Left Behind

Heaven Bound

Help Me Jesus

So we say with confidence,

"The Lord is my helper;
I will not be afraid.
What can man do to me?"

HEBREWS 13:6

Help Me Jesus

We need Jesus every day
Especially when trouble comes our way
All we have to do is say

Help Me Jesus

Jesus knows just what to do
Call on Him to help you through
He will come and rescue you

Help Me Jesus

Don't Ever Give Up
Don't Think Life's Done
Shout Loud And Clear
For The Holy One

Help Me
Jesus

Our Lord and Savior

Hungry For Revenge

"Do not seek revenge or bear a grudge against one of your people, but love your neighbor as yourself. I am the Lord."

Leviticus 19:18

Hungry For Revenge

Why

It's not up to you so don't even try

The next time someone treats you bad
And revenge is on your mind because you're mad

Don't start more trouble just do what's right
Call on the Lord He'll fight your fight

Let God Take Revenge

Do not take revenge, My friends
but leave room for God's wrath, for
it is written: "It is Mine to avenge:
I will repay," says the Lord

ROMANS 12:19

This is really good to know
Leave it up to God

He's In Control

Marriage: It's A Job

Therefore what God has joined together, let man not separate.

MARK 10:9

Marriage: It's A Job

Marriage is the hardest job a person
will ever face
And people walk out continuously

That's Such A Disgrace

They're not getting fired
Lay-offs aren't why
They're walking out
Because they Just Don't Try

Marriage truly is hard work
And it really does take two
If one decides to quit the marriage is THROUGH

Be Faithful to your marriage Loving and True

Do Not Let Anything Separate You

God didn't intend for us to separate

Stay Together With Love

Not Divide With Hate

Honor God's Vows

Need Directions

Direct me in the path of Your commands, for there I find delight.

PSALM 119:35

A voice came from the cloud, saying, "This is My Son, whom I have chosen; listen to Him."

LUKE 9:35

Need Directions

"Do not let your hearts be troubled."
Trust in God, trust also in Me.

JOHN 14:1

Are you lost and confused
Each and every day

Going around and around in that same old circle

Because you can't find your way

Need Directions

Follow My instructions
Listen and obey

I'm Your Savior

Jesus Christ

The Truth The Life And The Way

Now Is The Time

But as for me and my household we will serve the Lord.

JOSHUA 24:15

They replied, "Believe in the Lord Jesus, and you will be saved—you and your household."

ACTS 16:31

Now Is The Time

"You also must be ready, because the Son of Man will come at an hour when you do not expect Him."

LUKE 12:40

Now Is The Time

Whether we believe it or not
Jesus is coming back
Without even a thought

What are you going to do

Live for God
Or
Keep living for you

Now Is The Time

We have 24 hour days
Spend some time with God
Let Him show you His ways

Now Is The Time

Praise Him

Give thanks to the Lord, for He is good;
His love endures forever.

PSALM 118:1

My mouth will speak in praise
of the Lord.
Let every creature praise His holy name
forever and ever.

PSALM 145:21

For The Things He Has Done And Will Do! Part II

Praise Him

Praise Him before you rise from bed

Praise Him before you rest your head

Praise Him for things throughout the day

He loves it when He hears you say

Thank You Lord

God is our Father He cares for you

Praise Him daily is what we should do

He is my God, and I will praise Him,
My Father's God, and I will exalt Him.

EXODUS 15:2

When Praises Go Up

Blessings Come Down

The Answer

Everyone who has this hope in
Him purifies himself, just as
He is pure.

I JOHN 3:3

The Answer

Don't quit trying
When satan starts lying

Satan says: There is No Hope
Life's too hard and you Just Can't Cope

When life turns into a struggle
And you feel you can't go on........

All the strength in your body
It seems to All Be Gone

It really hurts so bad that you don't know what to do
Because your mind starts believing, what satan says is
True

The Answer

GOD

ROMANS 15:13

May the God of hope fill you with all joy and peace as you
trust in Him, so that you may overflow with
hope by the power of the Holy Spirit.

You Can Cope
Believe
There Is Always Hope

The Heart

Create in me a pure heart,
O God, and renew a steadfast spirit
within me

PSALM 51:10

The Heart

Have you ever wondered

What's wrong with me
My life's not what I want it to be

WELL

It's Surgery Time

Let God operate on you
Out with the old
In with the new

Your mind may tell you what to do

BUT

It's all about your heart
That gets you through

Get your surgery done today

Get It Done

GOD'S WAY

Satan Kills:

The thief comes only to steal, kill and destroy......

JOHN10:10

Jesus Heals:

Who forgives all your sins and heals all your diseases.....
PSALM 103:3

The Healer
(Anything At All)

.....for I am the Lord, who heals you.

EXODUS 15:26

Doctors tell us what they know
Give us some medicine and let us go
We hope for our healing who wants to be sick
Will the medicine be the cure
Will it really do the trick

The Healer
Jesus Christ

Heal me, O Lord, and I will be healed, save me and I will be saved, for You are the one I praise.

JEREMIAH 17:14

Anything At All

Don't Wait
Please Call: 1-800-Jesus Christ

PRAY

The Power of Prayer

Therefore I tell you, whatever you ask for in prayer, believe that
you have received it, and it will be yours.

Mark 11:24

The Power Of Prayer

Is any one of you in trouble?
He should pray.

JAMES 5:13

Do you believe in the Power of Prayer
OR
Maybe you really Just Don't Care

Tell me

Do you know of anything anywhere
That you can compare
To the Power of Prayer

WELL IS THERE

Try the Power of Prayer
What do you have to lose
It will be the best decision you will ever choose

Prayer Changes Things

IF WHAT YOU PRAY IS IN GOD'S WILL

COUNT IT ALL GOOD

BECAUSE

It's A Done Deal

Trust In The Lord
(Always Pray)

Trust in the Lord with all your heart and lean
not on your own understanding;
in all your ways acknowledge Him,
and He will make your paths straight.

PROVERBS 3:5-6

Trust In The Lord
(Always Pray)

Trust in the Lord and do good, dwell
in the land and enjoy safe pasture.

PSALM 37:3

Trust in the Lord Always Pray
Don't listen to satan when you hear him say

You're wasting your time when you Trust and Pray
Your prayers don't get answered anyway

Stop listening to satan

You may receive a miracle
Or
Maybe not

Still Trust In The Lord
With All You've Got

Heart
Mind
Soul

Trust and Pray

God Will Make A Way

Where Would I Be

O Lord my God,

I called to You for help and You healed me.

PSALM 30:2

O Lord my God, I will give You thanks forever.

PSALM 30:12

Where Would I Be

But I trust in You, O Lord
I say You are my God.

PSALM 31:14

Lord

I thought I knew
Just what to do
But my life changed
Following You

You show me what is right and wrong
When I am weak You make me strong

I will always trust in You
Because I know Your Word is True
This is something I must do
I will always trust in You

You walk with me
You talk with me

Without You Lord

Where Would I Be

Without A Doubt

Now faith is being sure of what we hope for and certain of what we do not see.

HEBREWS 11:1

Believing Without Seeing

Without A Doubt

"Have faith in God," Jesus answered.

MARK 11:22

Truly

All the faith you really need
Is only the size of a mustard seed

Where's your faith when trials come your way

Is it in God
To Him do you Pray

We may not see God one to one
Nor do we see Jesus His Begotten Son

But

That's what faith is all about
Believing without seeing

Without
A
Doubt

**Who Is This Man
(It Can Only Be)**

And a voice from Heaven said, "This is My
Son whom I Love;
with Him I am well pleased."

MATTHEW 3:17

Who Is This Man
(It Can Only Be)

Who is this Man people talk about
Who will return from Heaven

WITHOUT A DOUBT

Who Is This Man

He died on a cross
He shed His blood for you and me
He healed the lame to walk
He healed the blind to see

Who Is This Man

He walked on water
Gave life back to the dead

Love the Lord your God with all your heart
And
Love your neighbor as yourself
Are two things that He said

Who Is This Man

It Can Only Be
It Can Only Be

GOD'S ONLY BEGOTTEN SON

Jesus Christ
The Holy One

Who's Perfect

Be kind and compassionate to one another, forgiving each other, just as in Christ, God forgave you.

EPHESIANS 4:32

Who's Perfect

You're not perfect
Neither am I
We will never be perfect no matter
how hard we try

We will all make mistakes along the way
By what we do and what we say

If I hurt you or you hurt me
We must understand

It's A Possibility

Live And Forgive

"A new command I give you: Love one another. As I have loved you, so you must love one another."

JOHN 13:34

Now

This is said and it must be done
Spoken from The Only Perfect One

Jesus Christ

Who's The Judge

Do not show partiality in judging;
hear both small and great alike.

Do not be afraid of any man,
for judgment belongs to God.

Bring Me any case too hard for you,
and I will hear it.

DEUTERONOMY 1:17

Who's The Judge

Order in the court
All rise
You may be seated

Who's The Judge

We see people every day
They look different
They act different
In their own special way

Are we to judge them

Not At All

It's not up to us to make that call

Who's The Judge

GOD

There is only one Lawgiver and Judge,
the one who is able to save and destroy.
But you—who are you to judge
your neighbor?

JAMES 4:12

*Now You Know
So Let It Go*

Why

The Lord is good, a refuge in times
of trouble.
He cares for those who trust in Him.

NAHUM 1:7

This poem is dedicated to Ramon Boza.

People face problems every day
That's part of life, they're here to stay

Don't Give Up

Pray   Pray   Pray

P.U.S.H.
Pray
Until
Something
Happens

For The Things He Has Done And Will Do! Part II

Why

Why Lord Why
What did I do
I don't deserve what I'm going through

Every time I turn around
Something is always getting me down

Why

My Child

Don't Give Up

Bad things will sometimes happen to you
It doesn't matter what you do

I never promised life would always be fun
Look what happened to My Son

I will promise if you stay with Me
I'll take care of you

I GUARANTEE

God is our refuge and strength,
an ever-present help in trouble.

PSALM 46:1

In Closing

With God nothing is impossible

God says: HEBREWS 13:5

Never will I leave You
Never will I forsake You

That tells the love God has for you
Our love for Him should be the same too

People

Put God number one, and keep Him there
Everything else in this world doesn't even
Compare *NOTHING*

Trust in the Lord with all your heart
and lean not on your own understanding;
in all your ways acknowledge Him, and He will
make your paths straight.

Proverbs 3:5-6

*Always Believe
Don't Ever Give Up*

*May God Bless You
In Everything You Do*

AMEN and HALLELUJAH

About Michael Williams:

Michael Williams was born in a small town called Salina, located in the Sun Flower State of Kansas. He is 2nd youngest of five siblings, two boys and three girls. It was in 2003 when Michael received his calling to minister through poetry. Completing his first book *To God Be The Glory vol.1*, Michael actively ministered his publication in Kansas, at the local Churches.

In 2003 his oldest daughter, Season, relocated to Dallas, Texas faithfully following her husband, Pastor Derek Jacobs calling to ministry. It wasn't long after that Michael, his wife Michelle and 2 younger daughters soon followed. It was in Dallas that Michael Williams then faithfully completed the second of the two books, *To God Be The Glory vol. 2.*

Simple and precise poetry written so that all can easily get the message. "It has to be simple, because I want all readers both young and old to enjoy and understand God's word", explains the author Michael Williams. Whether it's the word or Michael's passion behind his delivery, that engages and moves anyone that attends his events.

"I was moved to tears when I heard Michael's poetry, it was just what I needed to hear and when I needed to hear it", exclaimed Ms. Green a Dallas teacher that attended one of Michael's events here in Dallas. She continued "I purchased one for each of my friends and my teen daughter, I knew she needed to hear *The Answer*."

CPSIA information can be obtained
at www.ICGtesting.com
Printed in the USA
FSOW01n1024281017
40310FS